HOMEWARD

HOMEWARD

— *poems* —

Elizabeth Keough McDonald

Homeward: poems
Copyright ©2013 Elizabeth Keough McDonald

ISBN: 978-0-9892882-0-0
Publisher: Mercury HeartLink
Printed in the United States of America

Portrait Photography by Brian Leddy
http://brianleddyphoto.photoshelter.com

Mercury HeartLink
www.heartlink.com
editor@heartlink.com

Acknowledgments

The works in this volume that have appeared in other publications are acknowledged as follows:

Powder: "Yes, Sir!", "To The Survivors", and "Every Night Is Footsteps".
Intensive Care: "The Politics of Disease" and " Bataan Angels".
Malpais Review Spring 2011: "Memorial Day"
Adobe Walls: "Ribbons".
Looking Back To Place: "Summer Vacation".
Crazy Woman Creek: "The Ramah Farmers' Market".
Very Large Array: "Refinery".
The Alembic: "Intrusion"
Harwood Anthology: "Route 66 Roundup"
Central Avenue: "Watchdog", " 4th Degree Felony", 'The Drummer", "Counting".
Connecticut Writers 1979: "Before I settle Down...(Autumn Cabin)".
American Journal Of Nursing: "Bataan Angels".
Blanket statements, Newsletter of the American Quilt Study Group: "The Seamstress"
Santa Fe New Mexican: "Dogs Versus Cats- Who Wins?"

Poems

Dedicated to my maternal grandmother,
Elizabeth T. Keough McGee.

A woman of wisdom, who knew the difference.

HOMEWARD

*Thank you to the many teachers
who have guided me
in my search for home.*

Never Shake the Mill

It was morning, and the factory bell
Had sent forth its early call,
And many a weary one was there,
Within the dull factory wall.
—Factory song from Lowell, MA

the downtrodden hang-dog of defeat.
A stupid Mick he called himself,
the Irish shanty-eye who could not
befriend his mother's voice or rid
his shoes of newspaper lining.
"I could have studied at the Sorbonne.
Been like Hemingway in Paris, but
I could never shake the mill", he crooned
between beers, "After the war," he told
me, "I had the GI Bill to study abroad,
but all I'm thinking is no father, so take
care of my mother."

In Pawtucket, Rhode Island he lived
with the slum, slung rack of workers,
hobbled for a dole and a pint. Married
to the long walk down piss alley, dog
gnash and the fist beat of a wife struck.
Light from cataract windows, yellowed the
pound and din of machinery—a rounded boot
stomp to the head. Lungs like magnets, cotton
fibers tortured with the cough and hack, washed
down with the river swill of a community bucket.
He figured he breathed in a gent's wardrobe a day.

Never shake the mill, even with education

and success. Like a rare haunting, the thin
film of ghost caught between twilight and dark,
the lunch whistle sounded when least expected.
Kicked him back to the bloody-handed fist of the drinking man.
No song in his heart.

The Seamstress

wrapped me in long bolts of fabric.
Swaddled me in play, gently, as a newborn.
She taught me color with canvas bags of scrap
fabric she saved for a quilt, a pillow, any rainy day
project. So I would remember their names, she told me
purple was like rain on the fire escape, yellow was quiet
in the company of noisy brothers, and red smelled like
the beach before the tide remembered it needed to hurry.

When I sewed next to her she would brush against
my fingers with a pin cushion wrapped around her
right wrist. She told me to tug, pull, slide, twist
the fabric. Pointed out how all this mattered,
how I would learn the old way, the way of her mother.
Use old army surplus blankets for quilt batting. Cut
up thrift store clothes, to make do with what's here.

"I don't' know much about the proper way to sew," she said.
"I do what I like." Wool coats she designed cascaded
from faux black fur collars the way a bride would
glide from the top of a glass stairway.

Years later, her quilts warmed me during long winters.
Wind howled, snow drifted in pointed hats along the
window sills. White was a tired, sneaky yawn caught by
bedtime.

TRUST

gambles on faith and all her friends in high places.

A statue of the Infant of Prague postures
on the fireplace mantel. So many pennies
placed under his outreached arms for
the wants of blessings unearned. He's
pushed against the wall like absolution
on demand. A plastic statue of Saint
Joseph remains buried under a pat of my
front yard grass, adding a spiritual component
to fertilizer containing 2.0 total nitrogen,
2.0 soluble potash and 2.0 available phosphate.
Every Sweet Briar rose becomes a fragrant intercession.
Black, wooden rosary beads my grandfather had
in his decided hands at his wake, now wait
in broken sections on my bedside table
like scattered sunflower seeds. The mass
card my younger brother chose for my father's
memorial service reads something about
going to rest for only a little while.
But anyone with some Irish in her knows
the part that does not rest, becomes a haunting.

Trust is the snake in the Garden of Eden.

Summer Vacation

There is the daily sacrament of rasp and chisel...
—Dorianne Laux, "Prayer", *Smoke*

Along the banks of the Connecticut,
shade tobacco grew leafy stalks
through the steaming lush of June
soil, the humid relative of Vietnam.
Culbro, Haas, Consolidated- the names
of tobacco farms in my river valley, offered
hard work, low wages and enough exhaustion
to keep my teenage mind off the ones lost
to the Mekong Delta, Tet Offensive and
in-country hostility.

Fourteen years old, I woke each morning
that summer to the bleary-eyed blush
of elder speak: saving money and discipline.
My hard hat decorated with flower-power
stickers and a lunch made for a sumo wrestler,
the four-thirty a.m. bus trekked down Enfield
Street and picked up every eligible teenage tobacco
worker Monday through Saturday until school would
crank out the thin metal hook of a new semester.

Taping electrical tape around thumbs and forefingers,
I would ride the bus and prepare for work. Each strip
of tape was protection against the steel horizontal
needle that I would use to sew tobacco leaves to
string and lath. Even now, as I write this, I have
replayed the motions of sewing perfectly with each
thrust through an invisible needle. If I sniff long
enough, the black, sticky nicotine smell is clear
as an exclamation point.

Bundles of fifty laths, I sewed for piece work-
nothing other than $1.25 an hour until I hit bundle
eight, then 80 cents extra, $1.60 extra for bundle nine.
We sewed in pairs, one female sewer on each side of the
three foot wide wooden table and shared one needle. The
sewing machine was a long constructed overhang that we
reached up to with each leaf sewn. We fought to hurry,
as each sewer's mistake cost the other time. Our
tabler stacked leaves under each elbow so we could
sew without stopping. It was on the tobacco farm
I learned to compete, the other name for endurance.

A hanger, always a guy, hung laths in the barn
eaves so they could dry into their intended use-
the outer coverings for cigars. I watched my peer's
chimpanzee maneuvers cool us as each layer of
leaf and lath crept downward. Occasionally a fall,
as a hanger would break an arm or leg, and hurl
debris onto our heads. The best days were to fill
a barn with tobacco and lull in the reverie of
darkness and damp, not talking as the lights
on the sewing machines became our church candles.

Early in the summer we worked the fields,
and wrapped string around the fledgling tobacco
plants to tie to a wire overhead. Stretched
on tiptoe, my transistor radio tied to my belt,
Diana Ross sped me on to the tune of *Love Child.*
I tried for piece work and to understand why Diana
thought a love child was only born to poverty.

And that summer Ronnie Mather came home
from Vietnam, after tying up loose ends,
post-war. I had sent him packages every
month filled with peanut butter, home-made

chocolate chip cookies, Kool-Aid and funny cards.
He volunteered as a fireman and saved a small
child in Troughton's old house, down by Pearl
Street, but my mother, a lifesaver herself,
well versed in CPR, wasn't called to his
parents' house across the street, the night
Ronnie choked on a chicken bone at dinner,
five months after returning home from the
stewed jungle and dying before anyone remembered
my mother's ability to bring the dead back to life.

With names like Cephus and Marietta,
North Carolina teens worked alongside us.
Bused in for the summer, their wages were
sent home and saved for sibling and parent
clothing and household items like a black
and white television. I remember being
surprised they were not working like I was
to save for college. They lived in barracks
on the farm and saved $5.00 a week for their
shopping trip to Bradlees on Saturday evening
to buy hair ties or jelly beans, stationary
and stamps. My first black friends, they were
older and laughed a lot. Everything seemed to
make them happy and I wondered why.

Striated green tobacco worms an inch thick
and more than four inches long, balanced
head on tail as they lurched at me from the
plants we tied. I was told to step on them
or bury them alive, but I usually placed them
on the bottom leaf of a tobacco plant with
all the reverence I could muster.

In the Connecticut River Valley, summer of

1970, I learned a job that counted hours
could be challenged by music and singing,
until the next bathroom break or drink
of water from the barrel on wheels. I learned
the nicotine glue that turned the hairs on my
arms black was the same nicotine that blotted
my parents' lungs. To prove this, my mother, laughing,
held an old t-shirt to her mouth and blew out the
cigarette smoke she had just inhaled, turning
the fabric brown with her forced air. I learned
that Ronnie Mather risked and lost and war set off
a rumble inside of me that would call my name twenty-one
years later. Working under the white gauze tobacco nets
and inside the slatted barn, high school became
a hammock between two worlds.

BEDTIME STORY

> *Time sheds her skin at night.*
> —Tina Carlson

The Jungle Books,—your choice for bedtime stories.

A mongoose named Rikki-tikki-tavi, and Mowgli, the wolf boy,
came to Conlin Drive when your voice ran on and on and on.
The street light, another white eye through a soundless hyena den.
Each lick of breeze, the flick of a python's slither.

The jungle pulsed her green and damp across my neck
in dire startle, while all things pesky, and full of itch and scratch,
droned close to my ears.

And always, my feet were sunk in wet. The slick and ooze
of humid rot, the place of vines and quicksand. As each
lioness walked on air, I reached again and again for heaven,
a thin strip of red coughed from the sun.

The tiger stalked, his hunger my demise. Not even the
wakening birds could change his mind. My pulse ticked
as he tracked. What saved me was the shot. The loud crack
of gunfire that dimmed the street light, quieted the breeze.

The Church of the Not-So-Happy-Girl-Scout

A couple of friends and I have been working
to get a church started. A place where people
can come to talk, sing and eat.
—N. Haverman, Gallup Journey, February, 2007

Talk

about nothing related to the Girl Scout Pledge
or how many cookies we sold door to door,
when child molesters were a fathom our
parents had not yet reached. So how could
a girl talk about the household pest who
would gnaw on her flesh at night?
Talk about the latest trip we would take with
Mrs. Lorraine Foley, the renegade Girl Scout
troop leader admonished by the Girl Scout
Council for unorthodox practices: trips to
Cape Cod, New York City, Niagara Falls.
We traveled where no Girl Scout from
Thompsonville, Connecticut ever before traveled.
Talk about who we could call back from the dead-
other than a girl's eclipsed heart. The Ouija board
became a sonar to locate our missing parts. Talk about
alleluias, hosannas, and heavenly hosts- the marrow
of our merit badges.

Sing

constantly as we hiked, cooked. Walked at night
to the outhouse arm in arm, terrified. Sing *One*
Hundred Bottles of Beer on the Wall, Jacob's
Ladder, Amazing Grace, and every Beatles' song

we could recite. Sing a cappella, sing loud, sing the
same songs over and over. Sing in a circle after dinner,
after performing the skits we wrote- many of them funny,
some cruel. Sing at the nursing home and the orphanage.
Sing to neighbors while Christmas caroling. Sing out of key-
because who cared! Smile and sing, sing tired and sing
away every lost soul in the world. Sing away a girl's
lost soul. Sing as if life offered you her untouched
hand and a sip of warm wine, not the valleys
of a fist or a chalice of stagnant water. Sing, sing,
for all a girl's worth. The devil's dark eye cast away.

Eat

all the time! Eat Sm'ores with too much chocolate,
too many marshmallows wedged between soggy graham
crackers. Eat everything we were served: salad, always
spaghetti and bread with more butter than a girl should be allowed.
The Church of the Not-So-Happy-Girl-Scout obeyed
the rule of over-indulgence, but no girl would freely admit
to counting every M&M she ate. Eat seconds and thirds,
the dark secrets of weight and calories. Eat dessert and
sneak dessert. Eat with friends, warm at long wooden tables.
Eat with birds and squirrels, chipmunks and salamanders,
the wild creatures who found us and those we found.
Eat under one roof, under the stars and under the fullest
moon a girl could wish for. Eat in candlelight, in silence and
in our sleeping bags together. Eat after a hike to the store:
Fritos and potato chips- the hallowed wafers of a girl's one
long baptism in the Church of the Not-So-Happy-Girl-Scout.

The Politics of Pain

Before the craze about tunnels, bridges,
white lights of a near-death experience,
my grandfather told the story about his
daughter Rose, who died at age 12 from
pneumonia. *I could tell she was happy*
and wanted me to come with her- be with
her on the other side of the path.

He told me he was in a TB sanitarium in upstate
New York, and had died. He said he'd been dead
awhile because he watched Rose for a long,
long time. *She had on a white dress. I couldn't*
feel any wind, but her clothes and her hair blew
like a breeze. He described how she looked
like a prayer and didn't seem to stand
on the ground, but floated in the air.

In the black and white photo of Rose on my desk,
she's eight to ten years old- stout, dressed
in black ankle boots, tights and a winter hat
shaped like a small, sideways boat. Her coat:
light colored with a flower on the right collar.
Framed against a building's corner, she clutches

her hands so only her pale knuckles show. No smile,
she looks off to the left- a face brave as any
soldier. When I asked my father about her, he
was a few beers into stories about being a kid.
He bit his lower lip and cried. My mother became
uncomfortable. I said, *Let's not.* Later, just the
two of us, he said, *Grandpa Bill saw Rose when*
he died in New York. I told him grandpa told me.

My father said, *No, you can't remember that right.*
He never told anyone but me. He folded a piece
of white paper into smaller and smaller squares.
What I know about her, my father said, *it stays*
right here. He pointed to his forehead, tapped hard
several times. Glared as if to dare me: his father,
Rose, what keeps us apart: the politics of pain.

COUNTING

started when beer cans in the wastebasket accumulated.
I counted three and you were on your fourth. I estimated you
would drink the six pack, then begin another.

In kindergarten I knew a simple mathematical equation:
increase in beer cans equaled the start of fights and
the vicious things you would do to hurt.

I counted cookies, chocolate chip and oatmeal.
Told everyone how many I'd eaten and how many
pieces of fudge and Christmas candy I consumed.

When a sibling refused food, lost too many pounds
and was hospitalized, I counted the days she was away.
My friend laughs at me for tracking the number of Girl Scout

cookies I've devoured, but I know the gauge to work with.
Five is a snack. Ten: I've crossed over.
Twenty equals many old hurts.

THE WEDDING

in Saint Patrick's Church, at the corner of Pearl and High
Streets with Tat's luncheonette and Gorley's beer and pool
hall up the way, went on its schedule as the cold heart of
the Connecticut River chiseled itself out of ice. What snow
there was flew on witch brooms, each swash of straw an
ice-pick.

I, so many years removed from hymn and praise, and the
Sunday morning wake-up of novena candles, watched miniature
men in black and white ring bells of sanctity, and recalled
that this house of God raised me- the flashlight child of nuns and
priests.

I, who watched my father escort the bride down the aisle of
my Communion, Confirmation, and all the jaunts to the altar
for the body and blood of someone who could not protect me,
saw him seared with arthritic pain as he lifted her veil and
then, tearfully, lost the battle not to miss her for evermore.

And the touch I should have offered to him then, as he
returned to his seat, the hug I stopped myself from giving,
was instead reached out by a neighbor man in the seat
behind. He placed his hand on my father's shoulder and
struck him softly several times as a football player would
console another in those pre-game prayer circles I have seen
on television.

I, who knew that this wedding would be the last happiness
served to my father in the wanton church of my lost soul,
the organ playing the posthumous voice of Mrs. O'Neil from
all the holy days of high mass and tedium, knew like he,
that today on his final power would he leave Saint Patrick's;

take in the stained-glass stations of the cross,
the pigeon-height, chandeliered ceilings. His eyes ebbed
light, my wedded sister the radiant beacon.

Five months later, the Connecticut wracked with flood, her
humid breath vapored the air, my father was coffined in
final state on the thin, tongue aisle of Saint Patrick's
Church. I, absent for the ceremony, watched the clock
in Gallup, New Mexico. Added two hours and saw
his funeral as I had five months earlier.
Every hidden hosanna, no sister to me.

THE CHAT CLUB

What I remember from my grandmother's wake
is the way her blue rayon dress slid off her
left shoulder and the rhinestone brooch I
never saw her wear, sunk into her breast.

Even her lipstick, which she applied
in better times as carefully as Faberge
would decorate a jeweled egg, was too wide
on her lips.

I could hear her tell the Chat Club,
the women only social group she created
in the 1930s for her poverty-infused buddies,
that the death dresser must have been off,

had a few drinks on the job, because my
grandmother's head, never bare for any
social event was uncovered;
unprepared for the party.

My Neighborhood Mother

a woman of the 1950s, recently died. She died easily, just
as her chortled laughs introduced her cigarette coughs in
my girlhood days. She always smoked- before, after, during.
This is what I remember: First came an autumn evening, late
in the woods. Along the Connecticut River with my best friend,
we lost our way. When found, this mother scolded, then served
hot food on a yellow Formica table under dim light.

Soon her happiness surfaced, the kind only nicotine
ignites. Cigarette lit, she eased back into a plastic
covered chair. Each drag, inhaled and exhaled without a word
in between. Haze kept our reunion at bay. She was a mother
shy of touch and wore affection like an apology.

This became what I know as contentment: A rushing river
widens its stance, rapids swing her hips. The bob and drown
of chance become a dealer's choice, and then the lull. My
neighborhood mother's voice a laugh. The thin knowledge that
a cough will follow. Float, I just float and the edge will
come to me.

Sisters Walk a Winter Beach

We walk close to the other.
Find sea shells intact and
well-washed sea glass.
No one else in sight.
The snow folds like
beach towels on the sand.

Tips of breakers curl and
reach the jetty edge of shore.
Brave gulls bob with the waves.
They do not chase after us
as their summer relatives do.
We do not talk. A sharp wind

cups her hand under our chins.
The wax and wane of ache
travels across the rising tide as
a lone ship rides a wide ocean.
Weather coming on island,
redeems us.

WEDDING BLUES

The loss of us
kneels on my chest.
You married. Joined the army.
Left for Germany.

Long talks shortened
to abbreviated letters.
I thought of you older
since you were so far away.

You surveyed tanks,
supervised enlisted men.
I waitressed near Cape Cod.

You were wet, cold,
filthy in muddy fields.
Your fatigues chapped
the inside of your knees.
Eyelash-thin cuts
splayed your skin.

Tonight I walked the jetty,
to watch barges fillet ocean
and sky. Talked to myself,
pretended we were on Narragansett
Beach, years earlier. Marriage
then, a far off night star.

But today you wed for life.
I remember you were the coat
gathered snugly and I was
the scarf wrapped in wind.

MOTHER

with dark circles under your eyes,
Saturday mornings, after your
twelve hour nursing shift you would
drive us, your children, three tiny
sea urchins, to the indoor pool
at a Protestant church in Springfield,
Massachusetts, a half hour from
our tucked-in home along the
Connecticut River valley.

Swimming lessons, a goal for you,
so your fledgling fish could follow
in your finsteps. You are lifeguard,
lifesaver, the one-time ocean mermaid.
We learn the perfect overhead stroke,
the hand flat against the chill morning air
in upstroke, the down stroke.
Cut the water, you instructed, *like
cutting glass.*

In complaint, we fought with each other
in the car like children do. And you,
mother, driver side window down,
smoked just-one-more-cigarette as your
breakfast, lunch and dinner, the inhaled
nutrients of fatigue and desperation. I knew
the brusque of cold water, the winter air, the drive
that seemed endless and the early awakening.
My jostles towards the younger siblings,
were what any sea creature would do
when the tides were unpredictable.

Now, when I raise my arm over my head
to push a stroke fast, perfect in execution,
my sleek body in the warm waters of
afternoon leisure, a memory like an undertow
pulls me into tears: my mother diving into cold water,
her arms tight against her ears, curved to break
the flat unforgiving entry, white bathing cap,
skirted suit, heavy thighs jiggle as I make fun
with friends of her jelly mottled legs. My words
lash at her like a shark.

As my goggles fill with chlorine and salt,
I backstroke, side crawl, freestyle, butterfly
through a bit of confession and baptism, the healing
bath of my perfect stroke, my arm outstretched
to slap a turn against the pool's end, my
legs aligned and then the arm in upstroke,

I cut the water like cutting glass.

THE THREE SISTERS

of the garden are corn, squash, and bean.
Corn grows tall to provide bean
an anchor. Squash covers the ground
so moisture, retained, can close
its lips around each precious root.

Sometimes bean, the thin arms of
need, tiptoes on the soft head of love,
to grasp with thirsty tendrils a mast
that bends in summer winds.

Sometimes corn, the straight and steady
comforted by the wrap of many hugs,
is an anchor from all directions. Steadied,
by constant raindrops nestled at her feet.

Sometimes squash, shaded by her tall sister
and clingy twin, can rest and enjoy the
coolness of her creation.

THE NURSE'S DAUGHTER

A quick assessment, the boring eyes
of a seasoned caregiver, zero in on
a cut, abrasion, abdominal stitch too
deep for a belly ache. Absolution
given- *Play Ball!*- for the lesser hurts.
A call made to her friend, a local doctor,
for fever, chills, lower right quadrant
pain of long duration. The house call
arranged through years of trust. She
caught a grimace like a first baseman
stretched into a ground ball. Astute,
she called herself the germ-cell cop.
Lowered her voice to talk like a New
York detective. Pretended she smoked
a stogie and swayed with a swagger. Made
me laugh when she saw the rash, the flushed
red face, lethargy in the eye of spitfire.
Her clinical demure cracked as she referenced
facts of disease catalogued in her brain.
I could tell by the way she slid her sweaty hands
along her slacks and did not order me into
snow boots. She knew by the way I put my arms,
limp around her neck, of *Mommy, Mommy,*
parched into her ear.

If she had been a painter mixing colors,
an eye for shape and texture, or an accountant
calculating equity funds, an eye for improved
assets, then I would have been dead, the doctor said.
She tells it: *I caught a fly ball, two outs, bases
loaded.*

DOING TIME

Every window on Alcatraz has a
view of San Francisco.
—Susanna Kaysen, *Girl Interrupted*

Five nights a week at 10:30 pm
my mother left the darkened foyer
of the house for work at the men's
maximum security prison clinic.
She'd smoke a cigarette, talk in low
tones, pull the curtain back from the
oval front door window, watching,
waiting for her ride to the Big House.

Good night and God bless you, we would
both say, and I would release her from
a girl's slight grasp, to our wave good-bye,
to the car's ghostly exhaust, another
wide-eyed night. My father, again, not home
from work, I'd look out the window and wonder
what new information I would know at daybreak
about my mother, my father.

In the morning, my dad is absent.
When my mother returns home,
dawn snoops over the trees. Through
fragmented sleep, I emerge to greet
her as she wraps me in a funny story
about what the prisoners did last night,
as if laughter could be a tourniquet.
They made hats for pigeons, she says.
This morning she saw a pigeon with a black
top hat sitting on the stop sign at the corner

by Gretchen's house. She said she had seen
a pigeon wearing a chef's hat and one
with a beret. *They superglue them*
to the pigeon's heads, she whispered.
Her eyes—double exclamation points.

How many nights I waited up for my mother
to go to work, watched for my father to
return home, I cannot count. Always I wished
to see a pigeon with a hat, flying carefree from
prison to prison, from the Big House to my house
carrying a message that asked, *Tell me what you see.*

EYE LEVEL

Written for my sister's wedding 12/23/00

The demigod Maui ascended Haleakala at night,
to slow the speed of the passing sun.

With a lasso reaching like a spider leg,
he caught the galloping ball of fire
as it rushed to open another day.

His intent, he told the orange beast:
to allow my mother time to dry her *tapa* cloth.
The sun agreed to slow his speed, lengthen
his day to honor the mother of Maui.

Today, I asked the same sun, no lasso needed,
as it loped through snow and cloud,
to gift this couple, Trish and Jeff,
not with the crawl of passing time-
no *tapa* cloth to dry, but with fine-grained

illumination to ascend, as hand holds hand,
and see each sun rise and set at eye level—
the simple grace of awe.

THE HITCHHIKER

We made the trip to Amarillo
so I could meet your dying father.

To introduce him to the woman I love,
you said. My chest hurt right then.

No need to elaborate, the visit, respectful.
It was the trip there and back- a little hell.

What I admired was the way we packed
the car- no hunger or thirst could touch us.

We rode in comfort- books on tape and
a jaunt to the Tucumcari museum.

It was the hitchhiker who troubled me.
My father, dead, six years, came along.

I resisted giving him a lift. It would be
better if he took a bus, swam the channel.

But there he was! Hunched beside the dog,
and you with your dad on your mind.

Our disagreements grew like worries-
yours, the future, mine, the past.

We made the trip to Amarillo,
so you could meet my dying father.

VAMPIRE

Time is hope I tell myself.
Every tick, every tock,
could be one flap, one flutter,
a stomp or plunge in the
direction of survival.

My land in a rural subdivision is one
more parcel of fence and survey points;
the loss of a mule deer's eye view;
a cinder carelessly released.

In my lifetime, I think not of advances,
but of losses. I live in the Time-Of-
The-Last. Hear the last of an empty night.
See the last of a dark sky. Smell the last
of what counts as a clean wind.
My grandmother witnessed the first
man on the moon.

Time is hope I tell myself.
Like saying *what goes around comes around.*
Or *if I am good, things will work out.*
When I was young, my father would grumble
an overture as if reading a palm:
Life is not fair, kiddo. Don't ever think it is.
Time lunches on my neck.

BICYCLING ACROSS CANADA

*The clouds are moving
to the left,* you said.

So we took our time, drank
another shot of rye whiskey
in our morning coffee.
Birds ring-a-linging.
Maybe it will rain.

A rainbow broke her neck
against this idle mountain.

As I rode my bicycle through
a spectrum of color, a veil
of mist speckled my skin.
Quiet is a whooshing sound.
Maybe I can die now.

Big herd of wapiti swapping stories
in the middle of the road.

Permission to pass, I asked,
when I slowed to their rear.
Antlers like candelabras,
up an down, back and forth.
Maybe there is no trespassing.

There's a small party with two
Canadians- a guy, a girl and me.
Then the girl leaves.

I am past Thunder Bay, Ontario,

in a trailer parked behind a store.
The land of good manners, because
he stops when I say no.
Maybe I will end here.

LINGER

October days,
and this ride
through
New Mexico,
Colorado,
Wyoming,
and South Dakota-
what I know
to be the
ponder of
what ails me.

The radio music
deft with ache,
clamps like
no tomorrow.
Maybe it's
the violin or
the trill at the
end of this
singer's voice.
What is small,
unlocks some big.

No amount of
prairie weave,
up and down
these hills, not
the piled snow
or the antelope grazing,
not even
this autumn sun

or the endless
drive, drive away,
can match my sputter.

The Orin, South Dakota
rest stop plays up the wind;
an endless rollick
headed towards
Hot Springs. I'll find
some hot coffee and
chocolate. The odometer
says I am further from
where I came, closer
to where I have to go.

HURRICANE BERTHA

The sea and her relatives,
sunken ships and sand dollars,
seahorses and fishes,
dance in their jolly depths
to celebrate Hurricane Bertha.

Trawler nets on vacation,
motorboat blades garaged,
the ocean, her white-streaked
hair thrown back in glee,
shakes her belly-dance.

INTRUSION

Gulliver, Michigan 1981

Tonight, the house is alone.
No one interprets the washings
of the stars, or the thick-lipped
silence of a fingernail moon.

Snow banks against the corner
window, as an Aladdin lamp hisses.
The stove gargles red-eyed coals;
ruby beetles puff ringlets of heat
throughout the house.

A rocker, empty hearted,
stares ahead. Nods
cautiously, as a sudden wind
tells the door to open.

Morning Runs Through the Rosebud Reservation

A brown owl fences through the air. I watch her sink
into a field as vanishing night heat yawns in streams.

At 5 a.m. I run by Spotted Tail's grave, but I detour
and do not run up the hill, by the burial site as usual.

This is a distant sighting, as the owl did not cross
from the right or the left, nor hoot three times.

The doe-eyed leaving moon squints down hard. *How many
times do I have to tell you,* she cautions.

Signs are prayers in disguise, the voices of many gods.

Autumn Cabin

Thompson, Michigan is home
to this three-roomed cabin
of quilted blankets. Swedish
ivy window climbs and nudges
against a kitchen sunrise.
Upstairs, cold wood bare-feets
me awake from feathers sunk
brass bed low. On a porch without
screens, I stretch, suck deeply the fog.

Wisps breeze by, comb autumn
with a twist, a turn. They bow
at my feet and tell where they have
slept the dark as the scent of dried
leaves is carried to my doorstep.
Above, whirring wings slice the sun,
take with them pulse and breath.

Honey,

I just want to be canonized a saint.
Just like the six up for sainthood
I read about in the newspaper.
I can't say I've worked any miracles
for the multitudes, the fish and loaves
type of situation, but me- I'm doing
a pretty good job of caring for my kids.
Since the husband left me- the same old story-
for the so much younger diva, well, things
have drastically changed. What is the saying
about life is what happens when you don't plan?
I never planned for this- a single parent with
three kids under ten. My brother and sister live
out-of-state and I've found out that friends took
his side because, honey, I don't have time for
smooth talking.

I think sainthood ought to be automatic for a woman like me.

I don't expect anything from the honor.
A long walk, alone, at dusk would work.
I can sort out my next move with that
little bit of magic, now that I'm a saint.

CROW DELIGHT

The red tail hawk is absent,
replaced this bristled morning
by two crows, common.
Beak on playful beak,
they sling raps to
each others' heads.
One wing lifts to banish.
Three hops along the
cross arm of a power line.

I cut into open canyon
with my dogs. Ahead
is a juniper bent in a
question mark. Amoeba-
shaped puddles are delicate,
frozen. So much play. The
neighborhood bully gone.
So much play.

CPR

Her tiny mouth opens
like a fish kissing
water's bottom. She
heaves for air when
I clear her airway.

As her fleshy hand
wraps my smallest finger,
she tells me she is more
than a laryngoscope, or
an endotracheal tube.

Her lips are blue
when I push two
fingers rhythmically
against her chest.
I circulate her mother's
arms, a grandmother's
kiss and a happy
toss into the air.

When river ice cracks
in spring, sunlight
stretches a long arm
through each fissure.
Baptism comes
in many forms.

THE SHOWDOWN

Laden and Leleh Binjani, 29 year old twins conjoined at the
head, died after more than 50 hours of surgery to separate them.
—The Gallup Independent, Gallup, New Mexico,
    7/11/2003

Three things struck me when I read
the newspaper article. Mainly,
with the eye of the Iraq war stalled
like a hurricane with bad directions,
heroine took on another meaning.

1.
THEY WALKED INTO THE OPERATING ROOM.

No gurney ride through double doors
or pre-op medication on board,
where usually every good-bye
is seen through the sound of
a foghorn. Instead, the surgical
suite threshold became a bowed head
to their raised fists.

2.
THEY STRUGGLED DURING SURGERY.

Was one twin changing her mind?
Thinking it is better to live
joined at the head than die
like a splintered chair leg.
A whimper from the end of a
tunnel drove the surgeons harder.
The lawman pulls his gun.

3.
THEY WERE BURIED IN SEPARATE CASKETS.

Not together in one coffin,
where they could be turned to face
the other for the first time.
Hands entwined, their chins
tilted upward to see:
heroine, heroine, heroine.

Dogs Versus Cats- Who Wins?

Goodness, gracious, me-oh-my!
Dogs versus cats, seems like a tie.
Monday evening dog by himself.

Tuesday comes without a bark,
I'm dogless in Santa Fe when my dog goes dark.
Wednesday sadness grips my soul,
six rescued ferals wait for a bowl.

Thursday reaps what Tuesday lost,
two snuggle indoor cats, asleep on my lap.
Friday rises fast with the sun,
Saturday's feelings still not done.

Who's best is what's missing.
Who wins has already come.

Patras, Greece

The bus twists its hips, shucks and jives
through roads narrow as a bracelet.

I watch two birds peck at the ground.
They seem large—ravens or turkey vultures?
Closer, they become small animals.

What is so black—small goats? two ponies?
They pull a white cart behind them.
Suddenly one stands straight, the other

moves up and down. Women wearing black dresses.
Sun-siphoned laborers, they slowly raise
arms toward us. With my hand out the window,

I wave back the smallest hula.

Summer Day, Vermillion, South Dakota

I pick flies too heavy to escape
from the screen door, throw
then outside. The tired day
weighs upon my shoulders.

Children play on dull-witted legs.
Drowned in sun, they move slowly
in their tight, burnt skin.

Sweat glues my arms to my desk.
When I reach for a pen, my skin
rips from the wood like Velcro.

My wish is to be lifted by a cold ocean
wave, tossed into the startled sea, taken
from South Dakota the way my fingers
toss flies from the screen door;
salvation a simple motion.

Follow Me

By 1993, the skeletons of two woolly mammoths and 46
Columbian mammoths had been unearthed. Not all skeletons
are complete, but all that include pelvises have been identified
as males.
—John Paul Gries, *Roadside Geology of South Dakota*

Boys will be boys,
like lemmings
into the sinkhole
they followed

the next one
and the next.
A saber-tooth
tiger and giant short-

faced bear thrown
in the mix. Yet I,
who love all things
fossilized am troubled

as I pry into the open
bed of their tomb,
bone upon bone
wracked with doom.

A femur, skull, the
jostled disarray of
death splayed adrift
in rock. Trapped in

their open casket, a
vapor of frantic breath
rises; too thin to see,
too thick to ignore.

-43 Degrees Fahrenheit

It is so cold
that when people
walk past me,
I can write my
name in their
trailing breath.

I seek haven
in a coffee shop.
Its windows cry
rivulets of condensed
steam. I enter.
Order coffee.
Grip my cup.

My fingers,
swollen fish sticks.
My nose,
a melting heart.

White Lilies

I brought these white flowers
from Gallup, New Mexico
to Homestead House in
Hermosa, South Dakota.
They traveled comfortably
in the rescue kit for stray
dogs and cats- nestled in
their crystal vase, midst
food, leashes and collars.
They were like a safe travel
medallion fragrant through
Denver traffic, Cheyenne,
Wyoming snow dust, and
the tussled Black Hill's
of the woolly mammoth and
all things fossilized.

As I left on this trip, you
reached these lilies to me
through your truck window.
Here, you said, *the bride
gave them to me.* Your hands-
short, thick, callused from
percussion, cradled what I want
to be six pedaled messengers:

Have a safe trip
I miss you already
Come back and I will be here
Stop and rest if you are tired
Angels on your pillow
I need to say more.

WATCHDOG

The newspaper reported how she hounded the police
to give the boy a decent burial. *He had been dead
all these years*, she said, *he needs to be at rest.*
No murderer accused, no parent forthcoming,
Dead in a garbage bag. Found in fetal position;
the shape a lima bean grows in water or a cat curls
into the arm of a couch. She took on the task of
buying a plot, inscribing a headstone, recruiting
a bagpiper to lead the procession. With clergy
and twenty-five attendees, the seven year old boy
was placed by praying hands in the waiting earth.
And she, knowing the value of home, gave him
an address. Welcome, to the table of family.

Six Months or Less

If I develop a disease with fatal
outcome, by God, I'll move to Oregon
where United States District Judge Robert Jones
can be my confessor and Attorney General John
Ashcroft won't tread.

I'll obtain my lethal dose of drugs
when I have documentation from
two physicians that I have less than
six months to make the request.

I won't have to die in a hospital bed.
The power of choice my down pillow.
My head nestled in the hands of God.

POLITICS OF DISEASE

She flew to Canada from Africa- sick, with cough and fever.
When hospitalized, she scared doctors and nurses. Placed
in a negative airflow room reserved for TB patients, she
became what experts could not rule out- the Ebola Virus.

The news accused a hemorrhagic killer from another land,
another people. Across the border came aftershocks of
invasion. Under their suits and crinolines, TV reporters
perspired heavily and murmured, *Aids, now Ebola.* The flat

mouthed accusations of coach mingled with first class-
us and them. Others, hat brims turned low over their eyes,
blocked out the gravity. When the virus is negative, a sigh
from those who know contagion: eenie meenie minie moe.

I have looked out enough windows to know what passes by,
enters.

THE LAST SECOND OF SUNLIGHT

If you walk enough, with your dogs
or alone—a pair of binoculars
clutched in your hand as if
a weapon against distance, then
you know the last second of sunlight-
how she runs her fingers along each
reluctant ponderosa, gently as if to
float their eyelids closed, cusping
arc of sun with arc of moon.

As tired air cools, its font the back draft
of so many daylight animals drawing their
cushions of sleep over their heads, then
you know the last second of sunlight- how
she gathers yawning rays, tucks each
slumbering creature goodnight with tendrils
of ebbing coal fire.

If you turn to gaze behind, find the scent
that has tapped your shoulder, then you know
the last second of sunlight- how she shakes
rugs of flowers and dauntless bees to the
ground, the grit of shaded nectar, heavy.

In eulogy, this last second of sunlight-
like a butterfly's genteel wing, falls
upon herself in somersaults, head to foot
as day enters dusk in continuous motion.

In baptism, this last second of sunlight
pours salvation's holy water over evening walks
and cleanses sight and scent. Your painter's
palette blessed with simple blooms of goodnight color.

Rescue Backlash

*Finally, after nine days of round-the clock flights, the Coast
Guard suspends its search for Rick Smith.*
—Sebastian Junger, *The Perfect Storm*

My God what a long way down. Eighty foot waves.
I want the top of a crest to ease me into
the frigid water. I want to say goodbye-
my wife, my baby, my buddies. No time.
No words. I use my eyes, my head to nod,
I am going first. Then I jump.

Drowning went like this. I knew when I
kneeled at the starboard door, sized up
the waves, felt the touch of my buddy's
arm around my shoulders- that I was ready,
strong. Everything else was loose change.

I knew when it came to: gravity acceleration,
the tonsils of hell screaming up at me, the
jump- the last decision I made- fifty miles an hour,
my body shot into the mouth of obscenity,
that my training rested on a trough or a crest.
My God brought concrete, not the lips of a kiss.

Omen

A large loose
bracelet of crows
lasso the housetop.

Angled wingspans
dive into currents
of ribbon air.

Festered wrongs
circle a sky,
vast as memory.

The Language of Dying

In clinical terms, I excel
at the hyperbole of catheters,
PIC lines, the matter-of-fact
information of IV push meds.

Bring me your dying, limp and
fatigued, gaunt in hospital garb,
starved, from the perils of nausea,
and I will unleash death-defying
acts of precision, accuracy the
minute fraction of one more drop
of Demerol, to ease your pain.

This time it's different, as I am your friend.
Your phone call is a whisper and you say
It is almost time. I decipher dinner may
be en route or death and this is how it
will end for us: murky water, no clarity.

POLITICS OF HEIGHT

From the high wire transformer
the power lines extend a view
of the hogbacks. But a sudden
explosion startles me to look
through binocular lenses and
see the black wings of a raven
caught in wires. Feathers startle
upright like teeth in a plastic comb.
On an adjacent power line, another raven
cries *corruk, corruk, corruk.* He circles
his dead friend through the wingspan
of house sparrow gossip:

Where were you when the explosion occurred?
Could you smell the burning feathers?
How did you feel to see an avian electrocution?

The desire for elevation reduced to details.

Let In the Knock

The warm rain and pure wind
Have just freed the willows from
The ice.
—Li Ch'ing Chao

So you are a house with a view,
a nest for sunsets, sunrises and
the everlasting reds and purples

that swoop across big sky, where
each room opens into another.
Wide arms cannot hold you.

Windows lit from inside show
themselves softly. Curtains, the
guardian angels of allure, drape.

There is a yard, a dog, a truck.
A place to wander, a paw to
hold, wheels to bring and return.

Then the fence like a hand,
palm-out that says *stop.* Or
maybe says *don't leave.*

The gravel driveway has a few
bumps and dips. Nothing for
a puddle to drink.

The roof is a plan in progress.
Its new color will light up
the drab of silence,

as you open the door and
let in the knock that you
have wondered about.

BLUE BOWL WITH ORANGES

Rossi Bright, Artist, *Blue Bowl With Oranges*, 8/12/2001

Simplicity: grandmothers in shoes
too big or candle wax left over
from a summer storm's blink, I think,

this bowl of fruit wears like an open-toed
sandal. Air of wanton luxury contained.
Color, pure. Shape, defined. Intent, enjoy.

Palm up, these oranges lounge in their
own blue ocean. Cupped in salt and sea,
they backstroke. School of brother fish

offer the crest of each sun risen wave,
flesh and living joy. A simple journey
of nourish. The only word: ahhh.

LET THE MUSIC ROLL

I understand when a poet is dumped
in a relationship of twice struck love,
one can end up in their musings about
a lone calf calling on the dusty plains
or the dog's water bowl empty and
salt crusted like an ocean lapped dry,
barren, forgotten.

When a drummer ends a relationship,
the lilt of sticks caress, drag, turn slight
to their edge. Brushes soften the dim light
of a restaurant up to its ankles in bar glasses
as cymbals jostle. A solo rolls, rolls, rolls.
A little too long.
A little too loud.

The Activist

By day she is a regular person.

Her activities appear normal. She stops in at Gallup
Printing to make a few copies, get a cup of coffee at Kelly's
Coffee House and mail a stack of postcards where she spends
a few moments to chat with Bob, the postal employee who seems
to like what he does. Working out of her house, she runs
a business. Even her clothes are non-descript. In the evening
she picks her cause:

To boycott the latest cabinet nominee or write to Cibola
Commissioners to eliminate cockfighting. Last night she
supported the library to take over Red Mesa Art Center,
and asked Senator Tom Udall to ban aerial coyote shooting.
Somehow, she thought the two were related. She makes a few
calls to friends, more focused activists. There are fewer people
to talk to about these issues since she decided not to waste

time on moaners and groaners, or the transient nurses, doctors,
and teachers. They are the ones who never register to vote
because they are only here for a few years. They remind her
of fish flopping out of a grizzly bear's mouth, or maybe the
blackened socket of an electrical short. So she small talks
at the printers, coffee house and post office.

By day she is a regular person.

TRA-LA-LA-LA-LA

I live in Santa Fe now,
living the life of O'Reilly.

Lattes on every corner,
tight-shirted men wear

more nipple than ass so
now I look them backwards.

It is different from the full
frontal dark eyes, concha belt,

boots, got to love
those Amarillo jeans,

I-see-you sunglasses,
tan baseball hat.

I visit Gallup now,
living life, letting go.

Bataan Angels

The nurses of Bataan and Corregidor were in every sense "at war" side by side with the men. The difference was they carried a battle dressing instead of a gun. They fought, and fought fiercely, to preserve life as everyone around them was bent on taking it. In that light Angels seemed just right.
—Elizabeth M. Norman, *We Band of Angels*

After they survived Bataan,
no small feat in the shadow
of the death march, the military
paraded their anorexic bodies,
bad teeth and unrecovered illnesses
before the families of dead infantrymen-
with hope that a nurse would remember: a
photo would jog memory of how their son
died. Was their father alone when it ended?
Did it take long? Can you tell me? Hours, days,
the nurses sat on wooden chairs, in oppressive halls.
Stood first in formation to salute the flag, listen
to the Star-Spangled Banner, hear the accolades of their
angelic heroism. Wracked with diarrhea, migraines, painful
joints and insomnia, they endured. They, too, had lost
husbands, brothers, fathers in the war. Family members
died while they were captive overseas. Their grief,
the flavor of a circus act, hustled on the back of
a Colonel's promotion. Former Prisoners of War,
the Bataan nurses walked a tightrope-juggled
balls of fire, swallowed the sharpest swords.
They were the greatest show on earth.

RIBBONS

South Dakota Public Radio tells this story
as I drive Route 79 in all her slick, frozen glory.
I know there is a poem in the unfolding drama
about loss and the great zone of the near-forgotten.

The Public Health Service had sent seventeen
infant, Native American brain stems to Boston
for a Sudden Infant Death Syndrome study.
A woman tells of bringing them home.

The tribe had agreed to let the little ones go
after death, to a place of study and learning.
Generosity as wide as these plains, as fierce
a gesture that turns water to ice, hosanna.

Ashes let loose in a windy homecoming,
fly from the urn in a long ribbon, gleeful
as kites on the breath of ancestors.
Seventeen glories race to the light.
The hills to my right percolate in fog.
I open the car window for a glimpse
of color; a fleck of rainbow or black
sooted dust with obsidian polish. Amen.

Running Off Unrequited Love

Some inner sky, some expanding blue in me
is birthing a new sun,
a star never before seen,
that is you and not you, me and more than me.
—Dale Harris, from "Promise Me", *Into Indigo*

Mile 1

The full moon fans the early morning
and 42 degrees Fahrenheit would be better
spent in bed. Time for gloves and earmuffs,
but I wear shorts, a light pullover and
t-shirt. My baseball cap rides the tips of
my ears and my love-jones is about to get
kicked by some serious physical discomfort.
My car key tied to my shoelace, I jog up the
hills of the sports complex to be on the move,
the everlasting, deep-gutted move that will temper
my marrow and re-adjust my errant molecules.

Mile 2

There's pain in my right ankle and I
breathe harder than I want to. Rocks
slide from under my feet and the glorious
moon floats on a pink-blue sky, a sure
recipe to abate the vision I have of you
with a woman. In the walkway, both of you,
behind dark sunglasses, stare ahead without
a word. Your dog, the dog I love, recognizes
me, but you pull her back to silence. Let there
be another kick-ass hill so I can suffer some more,
touch the ground, lift off the ground.

MILE 3

Hill after hill, rocks and sand, rabbits run
back and forth, the appetizers before I hit
the road and then the traffic rushes north
toward Tochatchi. I cruise my memory bank
into your bedroom territory and the dog takes a back
seat to you and her, to the quilt I made you for Christmas,
to you and her, and the quilt I made you for
Christmas, to you and her, and the god damn
quilt I made you for Christmas, to you and her,
the quilt, under the quilt, on top of the quilt, baby!
I kick it up another notch, much faster than I want.

MILE 4

Almost half way done with the run, I chug
it up the hill to the Catholic school, wave
to the statue of the Sacred Heart, turn
around and run down the same hill to do the
course a second time. I look in the ditch
by the road the entire way up this climb and ogle
all sorts of trash, plus a whole bale of hay that blocks
a drain. The distant hogbacks shoulder your house
as I run parallel, three streets south from your yard,
your beloved dog, the place you rest your tiredness.
I imagine candlelight and two figures, now one, not me.

MILE 5

Familiar territory, I run the steep hill again.
This time I can't remember how I got here. I day
dream and float as if in a hammock. I am back to you,
the woman, and the dog I love. I can hear the dog's leash
clink against her collar, you and the woman wear sunglasses.

I say hello to you, to her, and you both stare. I think someone
has to be the adult here and damn, it's me. The dream breaks into
harshness as I slip on a broken bottle and quick-step to the side.
A tremendous heaviness weighs on my chest. Christ, I could have
a friggin' heart attack. A larger than life crow swoops over
my sky, wings it up and lands on a light post to rest.

MILE 6

This is where I saw broken black-on-white pottery yesterday.
Now I see it everywhere as well as the braided kind. Smack in
the middle of a parking lot is a lost civilization. My thoughts
are calm. I decide to like the woman and him as much
as I can. Maybe I can unload them both if I do the loving-
kindness thing. No, I am not there yet. Possibly mile 8 will shift
me into the absolution gear, but not now. I take another climb
and the traffic starts again—whizzing, diesel fumes, a bland
woman talks on a cell phone.
I look across the hills that I have run twice now and nature
thoughts take over. Like a lunch-time sandwich, the moon
disappears to the west while the sun rises in the east and
I am the baloney in the middle.

MILE 7

So up the Catholic hill again. Maybe this time I will
reach forgiveness. After all, this is what I aim for;
to let myself, the woman, the guy I love,
off the hook. I am a flash of anger because my brain
thinks again. Maybe I need to run a little faster,
cause a little more pain to dissipate this fire. When I
reach the top of the hill, I am a tiny speck on one of
those satellite maps. I have eaten all the finger pointing
I can swallow. Now I go deeper into the valleys of my
childhood, as I run downhill facing the oncoming traffic.

I know the woman and the man I love,
are really what I know to be my fears.

MILE 8

I am now ungraciously sad. I would like to believe
the cold breeze of the run downhill causes my eyes to
water. But this is all about purging, so I cry and I don't
give a shit who sees me. I cry because
this is about the choices I made, the feelings I have,
the expectations of disarray made right. All the mistakes
I made, rolled into one big sloping sweep back to the sports
complex, up one last gravel climb. The woman
is about him and not me. The dog is not my dog
and the quilt is a gift given. After one hour
and forty minutes to kick my own ass, I will return
tomorrow, god damn starlit morning, to do it all again.
Until my run towards, beats my run away.

The Interview

Her husband ill
in the front room,
propped up on pillows,
welcomed me into their
home. The elderly wife,
a nurse, attended to his
comfort. I interviewed
her that day about her
stint as a World War II
army nurse in Europe.
She was also a graduate
of a hospital training
program, a near-extinct
education. We talked
about war: death, hunger,
filth and the respect of
the military man for her
profession. She told
of French mansions
being converted to
operating room suites
and surgeries lit by
chandelier candles,
the only source of light
to amputate legs, arms,
remove shell fragments.
She ended each rendition
with: *We did the best we could.*
For two hours she reflected
on setting up the first surgical
unit after the Normandy
Invasion, dancing with General

Patton, finding a love letter in the
pants pocket of a dead infantry
soldier. She recalled events
matter-of-fact, as if horrors
were cotton balls that blotted her
memory. We drank coffee, ate
sugar cookies through her
description of bombings that
popped out eyes, shattered faces.
She remembered working 48 hour
shifts. The Army's edict that
nurses look and act like
ladies hung like a scythe,
as Germans clear-cut French
villages. What ended the
interview was her hasty trip to
the bathroom as she began to sob.
Her mention of Yugoslav soldiers,
Babies, she said, *babies, ten and
twelve years old.* Fifty-three years
after the war these children, again,
took their last breath. When her
husband yelled he needed a cup
of tea, she returned to tell me
she was busy. *You will have to
leave now,* she said, and turned
her wedding ring quickly, as if
to screw the top closed on a
seeping, toxic substance.

Valentine's Day 2007

It seems someone always needs
more plant food than I require,
or more tepid water to spur
on new and gentle growth.

I have rearranged the roots
of tendril plants, their clustered
cling, kneaded open by my
knowing hand. I have guided
the unsure branches of a yearling
cottonwood towards the sun,
out of the harsh Gallup,
New Mexico winds.

Early bulbs, who have pushed through
semi-frozen ground, have warranted my
admiration and congratulation. The break
of color is a candle flicker in dry land.

Yet, what I want this Valentine's Day,
February 14th, 2007, is something
new, a globe willow possibly.
Content with adequate nutrients,
and moisture saved for lean years,
its rounded crown is established.

Dog Walk

The dogs flush out a 38D aquamarine bra.
Its tiny rose center and lace fringe brambled
in dirt. Three beer cans balance in the branches
of a twisted juniper, as a wind flails to loosen.
With a child's white sandal the dogs play tug-of-war,
then chug their noses in a pile of horse apples. When
the smallest dog runs toward me, a bleached rib bone
gripped in his smile, the sun sets like a blood-shot eye.

LIAR

I'm calling to make sure you got tested,
he said.
I'd feel terrible if anything happened to you.

Hepatitis C
STD
HIV

The banal highways of
denial,
deceit,
death.

Liar.

STRAYS

Animal noises—
short sharp breaths,
snorts, a flailing paw
scratch through Yuletide quiet.

Wrung like dish towels,
cats and dogs decorate
the couch. Precious
Christmas lights blown
astray- in from the cold,
from a Gallup, NM winter.

Each inhalation blesses the immediate.
Each exhalation forgives the past.

Blood Sport

Everyone's got a reason
that roosters should or should not tear
each other apart in Cibola County, New Mexico.
The meeting is heated and statements are sworn
on the Blessed Mother and mothers in general.
Some say cockfighting is a cultural landmark,
a question of heritage, machismo. Others say
cockfighting is inhumane and leads to domestic
violence. Then some say, cockfighting offers
the opportunity to run a business, keep feed
stores operating and increase revenue for the
local economy. The Others state it is a
blood sport and teaches children to hurt animals.

Not as bad as watching violence on TV, one spectator says.
They only make chicken noises, not screams like people do.
The man from out-of-state, the breeder, the one with the
paunchy belly, wants to help business in New Mexico.
Kids grow up just fine with cockfighting, a witness states.

In the magazine photos, one rooster wears a scapula around
his neck. Another, a champion, has a red jacket complete
with a hood and scarf, looking somewhere between a bunny
and a Barbie, the 2 inch gaffs absent. Glossy magazines
advertise breeds and pedigree. Cockfighting is legal in New
Mexico, Louisiana and Oklahoma. The meeting ends.
They say times are changing. The phase one vote banishes
cockfighting in Cibola County, New Mexico.

On the way to Albuquerque, I could stop and roll a few dice, play a couple of slots at Sky City Casino. There's a buffet, tourists. Everyone's got a reason to feel lucky tonight.

VETERAN

I have tried to hang the American flag
on holidays that make me happy,
like my birthday on the Fourth of July.
Seems standard enough, but the others,
Veterans' Day, are tough.

I have trouble with songs of heartbreak
strung along in verses, like lost socks
missing their mate. Of course, newspapers
don't help, with photos of Blue Star Mothers,
one-legged daughters, Iraq and Afghanistan
children bawling like wet cats. Please go away.

Sometimes the church pastor says,
Remember our troops. I know his intentions
are good, but thrown in with someone's knee
surgery or fender bender, a bout with cancer or
a special intention...well, I try to have compassion.

In my mind, I light a novena candle with a tiny wick
to show I have feelings for another's concerns. The
tears I hush from my face surprise me.
All I want the pastor to say is
I pray for all of you.

AMERICA THE BEAUTIFUL

A new day for Gallup.
—Mayor Bob Rosebrough, 2003

Plastic bags flap, inflate, deflate
on the hill behind Earl's restaurant.
Caught by prickly pear and wind-run
sage, they snap as towels would sting
human flesh. Like fragile headstones,
they pulsate irreverently. Give free
advertisement for Albertsons, Wal-Mart.

While the storm in this Gallup, New Mexico
sky bristles a five o'clock shadow, I think
Flanders Field, red poppies, a graveyard
unattended.

My salute, unobserved, seems proper.

A Sharp Place

She hears a remedy of lost sound
she believed was hers.
—Linda Hogan, from "Window In Stone", *Seeing*
Through The Sun

possibly not known as such,
is the rise of my hips. It juts
like a starved chin, full of pout
and the sass of desire: for a meal,
a morsel, the ambrosia of food.

Stronger than my hunger,
is discipline: how to
suck-it-up, tough-it-out,
get-over-it, the mantras
of the military that made
me a good soldier.

Comfort comes from the
feel of my skeleton, the
road of bones free from
overgrowth, weeds, and
the stray, deep-rooted plant.
Fat and muscle are debris.

Another casualty of war,
is the waistline of a sprite.
The angle of my silhouette
is new terrain to discover.
Would I disappear,
satiety would be mine.

ROUTE 66 ROUNDUP

The highway lassos Route 66.
Gallup: next four exits.
Enter by Denny's and the radiator shop,
or the El Rancho for some history.

Gallup: next four exits.
The third, Wal-Mart and Shiprock north,
or the El Rancho for some history.
On the west end, red rock skyscrapes.

The third, Wal-Mart and Shiprock north,
Enter by Denny's and the radiator shop,
On the west end, red rock skyscrapes.
The highway lassos Route 66.

DECISION

Who lives replaces
who dies.
Her pointed finger
is a weather-vane
seeking heat.
She casts aside the dying,
and deciphers imminent
from immediate.

Background noises-
litters bang on concrete,
a muted shout and
the rip of fabric
gently rock her.

God in fatigues
one soldier called her,
as a storm cloud cradled
his head.

THE DRUMMER

One day I walk in flowers
one day I walk on stones
Today I walk in hours
One day I shall be home
—Bruce Cockburn, One Day I Walk

When, and only if, you find
a rest is in store for you,
I will canteen-up a river
of cool water. Offer you
hands to drink from, be whole.

Or your feet tired from a patter
along rough terrain, so would I
braid corners and brief halts,
rounded bends. Whistle you
a flying carpet.

Possibly you hunger from
a change in diet, foods
turned-up-at-the-nose different
for you to choose, so I will cook
aromas for you to sleep in.

Oh! I would soften you like wax,
mold you a highway of venture.
Write you into every fairy tale
of happy endings. The princess
unravels light brown hair; takes
you easily through cinnamon air.

When, and only if, you find
a rest is in store for you.

The Ramah Farmers' Market

lured me an hour south of Gallup, New Mexico
every Saturday morning from late summer through
early autumn. With my friend Sherry, I watched
the Zuni Mountains yawn through sunrise.
Each bit of conversation shared was charged
with daylight lifting herself from the east.

Today, market vendors sit under cottonwood cover.
I purchase Flora's "Garden Silk" homemade soap.
Vicky's organic produce reaches from two long tables.
I pluck lettuce, beets, and tomatoes quickly before
they sell. Monica's "Swiss Bakery" treats, raspberry
chocolate cake and apple torte, accompanied by coffee
made by a woman with helper-kids, lull me into more
conversation with passing women- Kate, Lucia, Milagros.

Globe mallows, purple asters and the touch of chamisas'
yellow etch a path to the outhouse. The flip hand of
a passing wind cautions a cold nip. Across the road,
prairie dogs race and three horses do the same. The last
Saturday of Farmers' Market, today dawned in twenty-degree
temperatures. Good-byes bustled, I already miss the way
this morning began—women's hands giving, my hands receiving.

LET'S DANCE TOGETHER

They arrive in droves, motorcycled up
for the holiday extravaganza, the annual
Ride-To-The-Wall caravan stops
in Gallup, New Mexico where out-of-state
veterans seek welcome in dance.

Five circles—the drummers, then the dancing
veterans—Native American men adorned in feathers,
rattles and green fatigue pants and jackets;
the snakeskin that holds them back in time, to
Korea, Vietnam and now Iraq and Afghanistan.

The third circle stands stoic. Sways gently as each
foot lifts right then left in place, the women of the men,
shawls butterflied to their shoulders in colors
of Pendelton and the stars and stripes.
Plastic lawn chairs, coolers and hurried children

the fourth circle, then the fifth, the audience of
passersby, family, tourists and Harley veterans.
The latter, a circle of many smaller circles, those
with watchful eyes, others who concern themselves
with not belonging, those too removed to want to

remember. Then a veteran like me, who sold her
steel-toe boots and military clothing as yard sale
castoffs, where one woman's trash is another's treasure.
These are good for gardening, the buyer said.

We women veterans would dance together in the
Gourd Dance if one woman came forward, then
another and another. Close together we would honor

ourselves, honor the pretty shawl we might wear and
our regular clothing. Every turn of the circle,

our arms might stretch out like eagles; soar above
the huddle, slow step, the shuffle, hey, yah, yah, yah.
Nothing left to guard.

THIRTEEN DAYS AT ASPEN GUARD STATION

One darling bluebird atop the Chicken Creek signpost.

Two hours of solid rain
Three trucks pass after 3 a.m.
Four cups of coffee
Five short snorts from my little dog
Six times I've paced this cabin
Seven sows stare through the fence
Eight horses in a corral
Nine ATVs slough by in the storm
Ten cards I wrote to friends
Eleven hours of sleep
Twelve flies atop a cow pie

Thirteen blackbirds...no...
Thirteen West Mancos River rocks.

THREE HEARTS OF AN OCTOPUS

I try to understand
the mechanics of
three hearts.

Not the swish and thump
of the tick and tock
or the clean and wide
of an elastic lifeline.

Not the number of leaps
and bounds, sweat rivulets
and labored breaths
to get the pump and push

of low cholesterol,
low fat, all things
globby
down the drain.

What I learn from
octopi;
oh, yellow-eyed,
color changing,

eight legged,
brain-in-her-throat,
she of three hearts
invertebrate, is this:

two hearts,
then a third,
not mine, not yours,
ours.

REFINERY

Metallic hulk dressed in blinks
of red, silver gasps of steam.
A long white beard flows upward
toward Churchrock.

From the hogbacks it twinkles.
Shimmering lights tinsel
red rock feet, as winter's sun
eye-shadows a resting sky.

Then, a quickening steers
recognition of chastened rock.
Cathedral pinnacles pale
in this half-moon night.

Earth's blood sucked
into hungry tanks.
So many small hearts
ripped out in sacrifice.

Every Night Is Footsteps

The Other Woman
says *It can't be scary,*
because he only grabbed her,
stalked her, didn't rape her.
Didn't do anything more.

Her friend says *his grabs*
were violent and painful
the way he followed her,
unseen, in the dark, came
from behind and did it again
and again. So now every night
is footsteps.

The military promoted him.
He was such an outgoing
sort—a family man, Christian and
a team player. They decided the
four female officers who
complained about him were
simply, like the friend, "a bad lot".
Like overripe tomatoes in the garden,
who would bother with them?

One by one, her friend says, *we*
were denied promotion, split up
from the others by different shifts
and assignments. One sent to Alaska
and three left the military. A husband
wanted to kick his ass. Another said
he would kill him slowly.

The Other Woman says,
*Goddamn. That bothered
you guys? That was nothing.*

It Is Hard To Believe

on this September 11th, 2001
while the sun stretched her breakfast yawn,
my dogs beneath themselves
in the morning damp of chamisa
each romp unbridled, that a plan
to kill so many in New York,
and Washington, DC would unfold,
just as I tromped through another
slack-jawed arroyo to pull myself
into the glorious morning.
No thoughts going through my mind
other than, *Where are the dogs?*

In smaller death tolls, I have
examined where I was at the moment
of impact. What I was doing, wearing,
who I was with. The moment more than
the occurrence, is lightening to thunder.

A decade ago, in a military hospital,
along a hallway late at night, flashlight
in my right hand, I accounted for broken
bones, head injuries and the blinking wink
of a call light. Every plea for, *Can you help me?*
handkerchiefed a larger wound. The rape victim
assaulted by her own troops needed more than
a glass of water. The First Gulf War, 1991
becomes sorbet before dinner—will it be steak,
shrimp or the tender heart of veal?

MEMORIAL DAY

The yoga class ends with *Shivasina*,
and I relax like a starfish ankle deep
in sand. One baby ocean wave washes
over me, then another and another.

The teacher comes around with
aromotherapy and gently massages
my neck and head, her fingertips
trailed in rose oil. My forehead is
now a garden in bloom. My nostrils
wrapped in a dozen lover's blossoms.

The slow rise to a sit, my hands at
my heart, knuckles pressed into my
chest. We chant for health, and *Om*
and the special words the teacher
says as each class ends, *May all
beings be happy and free.*

Slowly I rise. Not a word in my mind,
only pictures of sea horses and Nemo
in the muted light of tide under sun. I sit
in the windowsill, close to another student
when I hear from her mouth moving,
Were you stationed overseas?
I return from my deep ocean,
turn to her and say, *Yes.*

Resurrected, my socks and shoes seem foreign
as I contemplate the question and my answer.
The moving mouth then says, *Were you more
overseas or in the States?*, and I slowly smile

and say, *Both*, and hope I can return her to
a quiet breeze and me to a deserted island.

Then she mentions last weekend's Memorial Day
festivities and tells me about Angel Fire, New Mexico,
the Navajo Code Talkers and the motorcycles
that converged. She launches into the National
Cemetery agenda, flags by the graves, until my
inner mermaid slaps her tail and I respond, practiced:
I don't do anything for Memorial Day.

Deftly, I return to my undersea cave,
to the flotilla of sea creatures decorated in glee
behind a reef of razor sharp coral. This morning
I became sea weed, a bud, a shimmering ball of fire
awakening to a butterfly. Now, as I get ready to
ride my bicycle home, my teacher says goodbye.
I forgot my helmet, I tell her. She waves and calls,
It's fun, sometimes, to ride without a helmet.

What I Want To Say

comes out in a language
of twisted starts
and false beginnings.
How are you doing?
masquerades for,
*Let me slide my hands
down your wide-planked
shoulders. A place where
you are imprisoned.*

You look pale, translates
into, *No one can unfold you
like I can. Let me show you
how I can call your blood cells
to rise up and shout!*
Baby, I know a little voodoo.

At times like this I want a
magic wand, a kite, a hammock
to hang between two maple trees.
*Let me baptize you with fingers
that talk, lift you in a drift of feathers,
cradle you, coo you.*

To say *I would shield you forever,
know second is really first,
look to the Almighty
and his orchestra of assistants
to sprinkle you with God
like extra parmesan cheese*

escapes me as: *It's funny how*

relationships work. I'm so proud of you.
Karma works in mysterious ways.
I speak English, a little French and German,
some Spanish, but I am best at the guarded
language of *come and sit by my woodstove.*

Aspen Eyes

Tree eyes look me
up my arms
down my legs
behind my ears.
Eyes of all shapes
and dimensions.
Tall eyes
low eyes,
eyes of a hawk,
eyes of a sloth,
three eyes open,
twelve eyes closed.
An eye coated in spider web,
another hollowed with bird.

Twenty eyes ahead of me
reach up for a hoop of sun.
Me, an eye blink
above ground,
call air my home,
soil my percolator.

The Gallup Wall

I've discovered a new power center.

It is the walkway between twelve glass
columns located in the Veterans' Plaza,
north of the McKinley County Courthouse.

Calling back lost souls of :
World War I
World War II
The Korean War
The Vietnam War
and two Gulf Wars.
Not to mention the
Navajo Code Talkers
Bataan Death Marchers
those Missing in Action
Prisoners of War
and Veterans, who have
been spent outside of war.

All Gave Some
Some Gave All
is inscribed at the end
or the beginning of this
somber pathway.

I am drawn to the families who look
for a particular name, like the child
who shouted, *Mom it's grandpa!*,
or the pensive lone figures who stare
at a column, longer than for just a look.

Sometimes, I walk at night when
the city is taken over by the next
flood of citizens, wanderers like me.
I am drawn like a compass to this
site as if a magnet pulls for solace.
The souls of those who *gave all*,
want to comfort in the best way
they know how. They lead me
to a huddle where the score is:
Duty up by five,
Honor, a glorious touchdown.
Country, abysmally short,
on the return kick.

The Royal House Of Jazz

*No matter what they do to you
don't ever let 'em see you cry.*
—Billie Holliday

Dig
the King,
a Count,
Earl and Prez,
Duke
of stompin' beat.

Suits and ties
all the guys,
make it sound
so sweet.

Then Lady
Day smoothes
the floor,
white
flower
in her
hair.

She woos
the court
with voice
and style,
the crowd
caught in her
lair.

Suits and ties
all the guys
make it sound
so sweet.

Lady Day
sings a song
haunting
in its
verse.
A tree,
some fruit,
she knew
you knew.
The lyrics
tell it
terse.

All the guys
suits and ties
make it sound
so sweet.

SEASCAPE DREAM

The wave
that kisses my ankles,
such cool lips.
Sand tussles my steps.

A breeze laughs yellow,
tickles my knees,
points its slender fingers
at cawing pines.
Branches rock
at the bite of the sun.

It seems
nothing is wrong.
Day will sprinkle dew,
share her flowers
with all who pass.

I want to lapse
into moonlight.
Put my handprint on
the face of the earth.

THIS DAY

> *You are the hero of this poem*
> —Dorianne Laux, from "Oh, The Water", *Smoke*

For Elspeth, July 7, 2007

Runs its course fueled by water and light
The Puerco runs amuck at Green and Second
Sunrise, another word for Aloha
There is java at the Coffee House

The Puerco runs amuck at Green and Second
So much wet, foot-loose and fancy-free
There is java at the Coffee House
Elspeth walks quickly through downtown

So much wet, foot-loose and fancy-free
Precious life, dew and firefly
Elspeth walks quickly through downtown
Meetings channel the hours

Precious life, dew and firefly
What is unknown can be discovered
Meetings channel the hours
Red rocks backbone Gallup

What is unknown can be discovered
Each invention a ticket to Paradise
Red rocks backbone Gallup
A new friend is a book unopened

Each invention a ticket to Paradise
Sunrise, another word for Aloha
A new friend is a book unopened
Runs its course fueled by water and light

HUMILITY

Katrina, my dog, kills a squirrel,
drops it at my feet.
Tail wags, ears perk
she won the chase.

I pick up the warm body.
Its neck droops over my fingers.
Yellow nails curved and long,
he is multi-colored:
brown, red, grey,
white and black.
A young male,
an early spring squirrel,
unschooled in escape.

I say my dogs' name
over and over.
I had forgotten
she is a hunter, a dog
who killed prairie dogs
and birds
to survive
before I found her
and she came to me.

She killed now,
to kill
and please,
me.

I place the squirrel
on the bluff's edge

too soon dead to be buried.
Let its fading warmth
linger in a rising sun.
Its youthful curse,
an old dog.

Yes, Sir!

> *...there's a sickness*
> *worse than the risk of death and that's*
> *forgetting what we shall never forget."*
> —Mary Oliver, from "Tecumseh", American Primitive

I sit quietly as you demonstrate
to this heartbroken airman,
father of a one month old child,
his soldier-wife sent to Iraq, how he
must miss fucking. You poke your middle
finger through the bottom of a Styrofoam
coffee cup and rub it quickly up and down.
After all, you are the senior officer.
The only woman in this group, I simply
look away and meet the airman in the eye.
I know he wants to cry, so I roll my eyes
upward as if this game is so-so boring.
I save him, but a piece of me drowns.

Yes, Sir!

When you call me into your office, the Chief
Nurse also present, to address why I would
think I need training in a field I have never
worked, you become angry and throw your
heavy pen at the table with enough force
for it to ricochet off my chest. I flinch
in pain. The black ink stains my shirt. The Chief
Nurse says, *That is enough* and asks me to leave.
Another military woman saves her man.

Yes, Sir!

Soon after, I am not promoted. I am unsure if this
is related to the pen or the complaint that me and
three nurse filed on you, the senior officer, who
thought groping us would better acquaint you
with the female troops. When you moved up from
Captain to Major, three of us left the military
and a fourth was sent to glacial Alaska.
Penance, a friend of cold places.

Yes, Sir!

My soon-to-be ex-husband,
a military man, calls me when he hears
my unit is mobilizing for war.
This is so exciting, he tells me.
His words become another
pen, Styrofoam cup, a stray hand
to my breast.

Yes, Sir!

To The Survivors

In the throes of a language I struggle
to understand, I hold my hands clasped
tightly on my lap, as if they would flap about
confused, or betray me.

Triggers, perpetrator, intrusive thoughts,
cognitive and *exposure groups,* the wretched
leftovers of *An Army Of One* and *A Few*
Good Men. Buckle up, buckaroo. My heart
the romp of a black steel toe boot.

As one of the female veterans in the
VA Women's Trauma Clinic, I learn
how to remember, so that I can forget.
I want to speak the tongue of my country:
the coded ache of what I carry.

Part of me wants to embrace the sorrows
that surround us. Shoulder for another woman
what burdens her. Part of me does not want
to know that any of us exist, because by giving
us a name, I call out to myself. The hole wider
than what I have closed.

BELLY REDROCKS

When I come out from
the University of New Mexico-
Gallup library, dodge the
end-of-day traffic with
the laze-headed afterglow
of book browsing, I catch
my head looking up. There
a series of finer clouds, scrape
the belly redrocks of Gallup.

Junker Bridge, Gallup, New Mexico

At night the bridge tries to break loose.

The arroyo underneath, a neighbor
to the East Aztec Baptist Church,
reaches up to push the road away-
a band across its chest. Some say
the bridge is haunted with ghosts.
Broken bottles wink under the
streetlights, glint, a flash of fangs.
Plastic and paper trash move
without a wind and fly upwards
like a cough. I drive across the
bridge as if to enter a tunnel.
Grip the smile of the steering
wheel. Look over my shoulder.

Keep balance, in the steady eye of the moon.

TREASURE HUNTER

His business card advertises:
bottle digger, actor, artist
and treasure hunter. A shifty
one-eyed pirate adorned with skull
and crossbones and the hungry wing
tips of several sea gulls blare out
from the parched, yellow card.
It beckons the adventurous into
a world unlike the nine-to-five.

His wares honor dead grandmothers,
upturned out-houses and isolated
dump sites. *I'll give you a deal,*
he says, his hand stretched over
a long table, as if calling the dead to rise.

The sun blows up and over, wind comes
straight on and across, parts the waters
of the next man's treasures clear to
a metal cheese grater, its corrosion
possibly a tetanus carrier. Cheese and
crackers become life and death.

His front-seat dog, no stranger
to the two-for-one deals, the let-me-
show-you techniques, hangs his front-seat
head from the car window, as if to measure
each sale in what it could bring him;
a bag of dry dog food, canned food or
a box of dog treats.

Saturday morning at the Gallup Flea Market
and powdered-sugar fingers tear at fry bread.
Kids run and chase. A parent calls a warning.
As each shopper passes his table,
the treasure hunter nods hello,
tenderly moves a cobalt bottle here,
a slightly chipped vase there.

4th Degree Felony

Nearly three-fourths of women studied, reported that
their male partners have killed or threatened to kill or
injure their pets, according to a 1998 study.
People for the Ethical Treatment of Animals—

Whoever commits extreme cruelty to animals is guilty
of a 4th degree felony...
New Mexico Animal Cruelty Law

She cringes.

The first stroke
cuts a long slit down
their pet rabbit's
belly. Him alive and
screaming. Blood flaps,
looks like drops of red
paint on my boys' shirts.
She holds their crying heads
close. Covers their ears with
cracked hands. I push the wet Bowie
under her chin. Mark her next.

She knows I will.

Amateur Detective Search

*Information from Lost and Found ads
in the Gallup Independent Newspaper,
August 23, 2001—*

I could invent a story or two
about the wedding ring lost at the
Gallup Indian Health Service ER
or Pal Joey's parking lot, especially
where it may have been lost first,
hospital or bar, bar or hospital.
In my story, it would matter.
And the grandmother's missing
medicine bag, faded light blue
with dark blue flowers. Sacred
healing items inside. How it
was misplaced, where, and if
anyone knows its contents.

I have searched the *Found* listings,
but no two-band, three-diamond ring
treasure reported, even with the big reward.
And the medicine bag, not a mention,
as if it traveled off on its own.
But there is a basset hound, female,
tan and white. Shan or Nello
can be contacted if this is your dog.

I've taken a poll of various readers
of these ads. With the wedding band,
most are concerned there was a fight,
an accident, a theft. Those polled about
the medicine bag want to help find the item.

Possibly call Janelle at one of two numbers given
and offer assistance. There is a feeling
the sacred items are old and treasured.

If I knew the time and weather conditions,
this could be a clue in locating the ring
and bag. Some history about the item would
help too. Most of all, an interview with the
person who placed the ad. Their feelings and
relationship to the object would be essential in
my story. And if they needed love, I would tell
them about the basset hound.

QUILTING BLUES

My rotary cutter slices
through fabric. The sundry
sorrows of my misplaced
good deeds manipulate
every quick wrist stroke.

Helping, helping, helping-
I have volunteered with
the best of them, making
quilts for the battered
families shelter, giving
them away to friends of friends.
At times, no one known to me.

Flying Geese, Ohio Stars,
Double Wedding Ring, The
traditional patterns of
many-women-speak. I sew
to stitch myself together like
I would darn a hole in a sock.

I know what I need to do,
but this purge cannot be done
in one swift motion. Straight lines
spew from my sewing machine.
Every stitch a gasp closer
to living.

Veterans Administration Hospital Waiting Room

I prefer to stand, lean
against the wall by a corner
and watch the woman
of the man elbow up to the
desk of Clinic B, demand
to see the eternal,
love-of-god someone,
who will by-jesus, help
my husband because
I have waited too long.

Then I eye the husband,
the veteran. He looks out
over his newspaper,
fat-assed and paunched,
not so many years between us.
I look him down the road
of where he used to be, with me
and the other vets,
the men in chairs by his side.

He sighs, surrendered.

BLOWHOLE

The telephone rings, constant.
Two weeks, then three, this
Private Caller surfaces
into my home with leaps
and jumps from an ocean
of distance, blowing wet
salty air like a lost whale
stranded in harbor, circling
each room of my house
frantic, for open sea.

Morning, afternoon, evening
each call disrupts and I
harpoon in hand, buoyed
by the thinnest slant of winter
light, stand ready to strike: tow
the beast boat side then kill
with my lance. But lovely
is nature, as exhaustion
extinguishes the slap of tail,
the big blowhole of sound.

SHE REACHED HER BREAKING POINT

my mother told me,
when I mentioned
the woman in the store
who screamed "shut up"
to her three kids in the check-out line.

Did you ever reach yours?
I wanted to ask my mother,
so she could explain if this was why,
when I was a child, she made
my brother, in his peanut
shell armor go to his
room, get dressed
in his jacket and pants,
fill his suitcase with overnight
clothes, as she got her coat,
keys and pocketbook,
to drive him to the *Lying House.*

His fibbing-filled head bigger in
such grown-up clothing and his black
eyeglasses so definite, I knew this would be
the end. *Myrtle, with a nail at the end
of a stick would be waiting*, my mother
told us, *and you just wait, you just wait.*

www.ingramcontent.com/pod-product-compliance
Lightning Source LLC
Chambersburg PA
CBHW020911090426
42736CB00008B/575